All That Keeps Me

poems by

Tracy Rice Weber

Finishing Line Press
Georgetown, Kentucky

All That Keeps Me

ACKNOWLEDGMENTS

Sincere thanks to the journals in which earlier forms of these poems first
appeared:

Barely South Review: "Simple Comfort"
Bangalore Review: "Not a Lion"
River River: "After Chemo"

Publisher: Leah Huete de Maines
Editor: Christen Kincaid
Cover Art: "Collage Sketches: Page 81" by Christi Lynn Harris
Author Photo: Allen M. Weber
Cover Design: Elizabeth Maines McCleavy

Order online: www.finishinglinepress.com
also available on amazon.com

Author inquiries and mail orders:
Finishing Line Press
PO Box 1626
Georgetown, Kentucky 40324
USA

Table of Contents

For AMW

Blink

Our Weekly Reader explained, they use oxygen with luciferin
        to produce light without heat. Somebody's going to die,
grandmothers warned, if one flies into the house. I knew it
        took a good twelve or more to light up an empty jar.

At dusk after school let out for summer, we ran barefoot on clay
        banks of a creek to catch them, a competition for luminary
points. Before neighbor boys mixed in, simple communion
        was enough. Under pines, we waited to charm one from night,

land on an outstretched hand, crawl across our palms, down fingers
        open wings and lift off, returning to the dance.
Miss Mead told class their blinks attracted mates. Even then
        I considered the hazard of making sparks, oblivious

reaction, without heat and without trying.
        It was Down-the-Street Boy who gave me my first ring.
Catching my elbow, he plucked the firefly from my finger,
        pinched its black head and, privileged

as a surgeon, separated luminous jelly from abdomen,
        rubbing his sticky crime against my knuckle.
Along the creek, girls with glowing fingers played tag on damp clover.
        By September, we barely noticed they were gone.

On a beach two hours after the school dance

you didn't know his middle name (Edwin)
or favorite color (yellow like a blinking caution
light you might drive under, kissing your thumb
to the roof for luck.) His Chevy Impala with whip-
lash antenna. Zeppelin blaring, windows rolled
down, he drove faster than he should've. Wind
tangled your hair across your face so it was hard

to see where you were going. In eleventh grade
he was your date and you held your ground;
then, you were still just a new girl. You thought
love worked this way, in a tent late at night—a secret.
Sand stinging your face and legs, you remember
how it found you when finally he opened the flap;
the outer banks colder than you'd expected.

Doves

It might've been because we wanted boys
to think of us as fighters, not lip-glossed
sweethearts in monogrammed sweaters.

It was the season for hunting birds,
but those sorority girls viewed us with
contempt—hoi polloi in flannel shirts.

Crouching among late September weeds,
we'd avoid our turn to take a shot. Gray
geometry of dusk, an augury. What

could they feed besides ego? At the party,
olive branch decoys: single bites of consolation
lined on a grill. My college roommate lit

two smokes, passing one to me.
Frat boys rehearsed lies, sucking
their fingers as live coals died.

Because of a Michigan Farm Boy

Golden apples in the garden:
while Atlas went for the prize,
      Hercules held the weight of wanting.
      A wedding present to Zeus from Hera.

When he asked me to meet his family,
I'd never seen a Great Lake. In winter,
      Michigan orchards whispered—white
      branches reaching for another season.

There were hardwoods
and quiet waterways
      he wanted to show me
      between Braeburn orchards.

He pointed to the trees
on Understory Farm
      remembering what he'd stolen—
      a broken place in the fence.

Making pies with a grandmother
after school, September
      birthday candles'
      golden crust.

For a sapling to survive
you must wait for the last
      hard frost before planting.
      In Michigan, spring takes forever.

Eve wanted to sample all
things living. Why wouldn't she
      want to taste the sweet flesh?
      Why wouldn't she give in?

All That Keeps Me

I didn't expect to find
      grief standing on the steps,
the porch light burned out,
      no moon; my brother's breath
slanting past me in italics,
      his news holding onto
an empty glass. Where
      was the messenger going
he hadn't already been?
      I heard my voice: *Did he
kill her?* My parents
      had finally arrived
on the right street: a green lawn,
      country club invitations—
every box checked.

      I didn't expect to feel
drunk with relief. Days later
      I'd find myself back
in my old room: a playpen where
      baby boys slept, a husband
snoring under the lace
      canopy of my childhood.
When the house was still,
      I tiptoed down into their dark
garage to sit where he made
      his last decision. What
distance left before
      I lay down blame? There
are fathers and mothers for every
      space left in me.

On the Anniversary of Your Death

Winter holds its place here. Foolish
daffodils push against frozen ground,
       work the odds they'll find spring

on the other side. By sunlight that's come
early across the kitchen's unswept floor,
       I can tell: soon your ghost will leave us

again. Father, take your shirts and
their salty smell. Take the memory
       of phone chats, of valentine mail. Take

your hands that pat my hand. Your fixing
hands: the bike, the wagon, the car, the camera,
       the cut. But I have lunches to pack:

ham and cheese, butter and honey, apples, brown
bags with names and smiley faces. I am
       your daughter, the foreman

of pressed pants, matching socks, hair
combed smooth so a family can run
       its tracks from home to school to work.

Still, there's time to notice buds
on Bradford pear trees, press chapped
       lips together, examine these mother hands—

tools, not ornaments. And you, there
in your garage, on a mission to mend
       all that's broken: unwinding

the hose, turning the ignition, rolling
up the window; your fixing hands—
       doing what they could.

Another Suicide in the Family

Despite evidence, the family
wanted to believe he was

murdered in the detached
garage, there to change

the oil in his ex-fiancée's car,
too low to drive anywhere

farther than the marina
where he worked his days

off, selling live bait and line,
rope for rigging and mooring.

To think she cut him loose
even after he'd pulled up

stakes; moved south to help her
raise another man's child. Gave her

his truck keys for the double feature
in town, along with his last twenty.

For the Love of Plastic Acorn Capsules
from Gumball Machines

In this one you found empty space
        salty erasers for every pencil in your case
        a formation of birds pointing you home
        smiling starfish and an entire ocean
        a lilac bush in bloom
        and the dream of flying.

In this one a cloudy sky
        a runaway balloon on a road less travelled
        your mother's love
        bandage for a bleeding wound
        just a sliver of the great big moon.

At what point did you want only the coin to fit the slot
        at what point lost the want
        of wanting?

When was there no more
        awe no more magic in what might
        roll down the silver chute
        to your cupped hands waiting?

Not a Lion

1

The fifteen-month-old climbs the winding staircase
of their duplex to the small bedroom he shares with
his two-year-old brother. The father is close behind,
his hands ready to catch should Baby stumble. Brother
has climbed ahead and shouts from his big boy bed,
I win! The small window at the top of the stair filters
early afternoon light onto Baby's white-blond hair. They
have just come back from a check-up. The father will call
the mother at work to tell her everything went fine. Baby
is in the top percentile for height and weight. He is mostly
on target with milestones. Baby and Brother will sing
the alphabet song with their father. He will read
three books. This is their ritual before naptime.

He said *mama* and
dada and then he didn't.
The seizures began.

2

The doctor meets them at the Children's Clinic
on a Saturday. He is the doctor on call. He wears
a patient smile and Bermuda shorts. He tells the mother
and father it's common for new parents to overthink
new behaviors. Baby is just unsteady on his feet, losing
his balance then catching himself. Maybe he is weak, still
getting over a cold. Is he up to date on shots? Yes, yes.
Brother sits on the examining room floor and reads aloud
Ten Apples Up on Top. Baby sneezes. *Bess you,* Brother says
without looking up from the book. The father nods
his head at the doctor. The mother gathers her brow. When they
carry the boys back out into the brightness of the parking
lot, she will say to the father, *There. Did you see that?*
Like a tic. He did it again.

At the hospital
a kindly neurologist
advises them to pray.

3

After a battery of tests rules out tumors and brain injury, the pediatric
neurologist warns the mother and father there may be language delay.
Delay gives way to loss. For months, few words. None spontaneous.
Baby mimics sounds that have rhythm. The mother and father sing
Disney songs to fit every here and now. They mount a language board
to the kitchen wall: words he once used, words they would bring back,
words they would teach him. Now Brother is three. Baby plays
alongside, not with. A friend of the family utters the word,
Autism, as casual as weather. The mother will research. A light
will die in her. For days she will not be able to swallow.
While she crushes half a tablet into powder with the back
of a spoon, Baby pushes a step stool across black and white
tiles of their kitchen floor to climb up and watch her
at the counter. He loves applesauce; she always puts
the crushed tablet in applesauce. After he sees her sprinkle
the powder, he will not eat it again.

A counselor comes
to answer questions. *In time
he may say your names.*

4

The mother calls a friend who lives in a big house in a fancy
neighborhood with connections. She tells her friend maybe
Baby just has a mind of his own. That he refuses to jump
through hoops. Brother hears her on the phone, interrupts
to remind her that Baby won't jump through hoops because,
He knows he's not a lion. The mother's connection gets Baby
a screening appointment from the city school system making
him eligible for special education preschool. Their friend says
Don't think of the label as negative. It's a way to get services
early so he may not need them later. On his first IEP,
the diagnosis reads, *PDD NOS,* which means *We don't know.*
Six weeks before Baby turns three, a big orange bus picks him
up on the narrow street in front of their duplex. The father
straps Brother into the car and follows the school bus through
all its stops all the way to school. He watches Baby
as the attendant helps him climb off the bus. He watches Baby
as his teacher takes him by the hand and leads him inside.
He will drive home biting his lip. He will call the mother at work
to tell her he saw Baby get to school just fine. He will tell her Baby
did not cry; but the mother will hang up the phone and she will cry.

Goals become measured
in clinical terms. He knows
more than he can say.

5

Baby is now a Boy. When the parents go to his preschool
end-of-year assembly, the Boy bends down to admire
a classmate's baby sister sleeping in a carrier. Teacher says
the Boy likes babies. That maybe the parents should have
one more. Brother cries and cries, *Not another one*, when
they tell him he'll soon have another baby brother. The Boy
uses phrases from videos to communicate wants and needs,
his frustrations and his sense of humor. The parents think
this shows how smart he is to borrow language in such a way.
The doctors call it, *echolalia*. Every night, the mother tucks
in her boys. Brother says, *Good night, Mommy*. The Boy whispers,
Good night, Sweetie. When she says, *I love you*, he mimics
her intonation. He has never said *I love you* without prompting.

The mother wonders
Will the New Baby learn words
before the Boy does?

6

It is before the world is on social media. The internet is young.
The Boy is now in kindergarten. He has been labeled. The mother
and father consider the buzz from other parents, from friends, from
newspapers and magazines and television. They hear about children
who are "cured" of autism. They buy books. They research special diets
and special supplements and special therapies. They take off work,
put the whole family in the car, drive two hours to a pediatrician
in another city. From her, they buy expensive supplements
to detox the Boy's "leaky gut." They take him off dairy; they take him
off gluten. This, in a time when special diet foods aren't available
in mainstream stores. Nothing is covered by insurance, but
they have to try everything. *Everything.*

And then it happens.
Without prompting he hugs her,
I love you, Mommy.

7

The Boy is five. He still uses television and movie scripts to express
complex feelings. He is able to tell them what he wants. He is able
to greet them all by name. He learns to write the alphabet
with a paintbrush. He helps the parents with the Baby Brother.
He plays with Older Brother. He loves to sing. One day, he will
surprise the mother, pressing his own syntax into a sentence
of beauty and awareness. She is boiling spaghetti for supper.
He stands at the stove and watches steam rising from the big
pot. *The sky is cooking Mommy*, he points. *The sky...is cooking.*

To be a poet
without words. He finds a way
to tender his song.

Simple Comfort

After the appointment I look up the word
because I need to find a loophole,

create an escape from misunderstanding; but
dictionaries won't lie

even when I'm desperate
for the good omens

God and Webster might provide.
How does *pervasive* stack blocks against time?

Isn't he alphabet-singing earlier than most,
just as his brother did? What

kind of grief can ease the headwind they say
language will bring? Small miracle:

metric feet have walked us this far.
Now we begin again. A rebirth

of sorts—the pieces scattered, a jigsaw
puzzle impossible to assemble.

Questions should come with answer keys.
Remind me again how lucky we are.

Say *developmental disorder* with a full, clear
throat. Mention the ticker tape parade

under which we all march, wondering in
vain whether we might be spared. It could be

worse. Assuming divine insight may take
x-rays of the fracture, conjure logical formulas before I

yaw toward a calculus of changed values, thinking
zero plus anything would be enough.

Leveled

When you picked him   up at school for another
  doctor's appointment   you found him
    on the playground   his mainstream

class running   laps to burn   off their third-grade
  energy   before going   back to the cruelty
    of seat work.

That time   you saw him   running among
  neurotypical peers   blond hair whipping back
    from his high brow   in late afternoon

sun. That time   on the blacktop   he was more
  beautiful than all   the others   body lithe
    unfettered   as wind.

Pawn

You've made this list before, still you're compelled
to write it: milk, bread, bracelets. You slide gold
bangles from your wrist; place them on the counter—
a scene recalling the O. Henry story you read in school.

You ask, *How much are they worth?* The young man shifts
in his Doc Martens. You wonder if his nose ring was purchased
in-house, originally a set of two from somebody's
once-upon-a-jewelry-box maybe bartered by a thief.

Maybe everything is bartered in the end. You wished
you'd gone to another neighborhood, another town. Not here
beside your favorite Food Lion. A plump woman, heavy foundation
and penciled brows, sits at a metal desk behind him. Perhaps

she is his mother. This transaction might feel less dubious if it were
a family business. *These are family pieces*, you hear yourself say
and bite your lip, avoiding reflection in the mirrored wall.
He tests heirlooms with a magnet, disinterested. Turns them over

to the woman at the desk. She makes a list with the nub of a pencil;
without looking up, offers your grandmother's engraved initials
to the scale, Muzak—the soundtrack of betrayal. The sun
beats through the shop window. You drag a sleeve

across your face, ask if it's hot in here. *Gets hot around
this time,* the woman says. You leave with the cash to buy
a week's groceries, holding the bills in your pocket
like a love letter you're anxious to read again.

Balancing Act

Autism doesn't keep
        my eighteen-year-old son,
                my shopping wingman,
from understanding how
        these kinds of awkward
                episodes unfold. We retreat
from Checkout Line 4,
        abandon our cart of
                bagged groceries to find
a bunker in the privacy
        of the family van
                where I am grateful
for the miracle of
        Consumers Cellular
                and dial 1-800 numbers
on the back of every
        charge card I carry
                to find one
not currently maxed.
        Resigned, I pull
                from a glove box

emergency arsenal:
        a few crumpled bills.
                Back at the cash register,
I finger nickels and dimes
        toward the adjusted total,
                its minimized bounty.
The cheerful checkout clerk's
        crucifix earrings dangle,
                her shoulders
not yet burdened
        with the weight of compromise.
                She feels compelled

to share the wisdom of her
  Sunday morning devotion:
    The Lord provides—
though today
  the Lord doesn't see the need
    to provide a box
of Chardonnay,
  a Boston Butt, a bag of Cheetos.
    I consider the adventure

whenever I pull our cart up
  to a check out,
    my tank needling E.
I mean, who needs sky-
  diving or rock-
    climbing or even
a summer pass
  to a theme park with such
    domestic thrills to be had?
God only knows.
  Counting on mercy again
    from the bottom of my purse,
we seal the deal
  when Checkout Girl
    hands over my
receipt with instructions
  to *be blessed* as if
    she'd lost faith
in *Have a nice day—*
  that smiley face stamped
    off center on two plastic bags.

Another Passage

I brought for her bedside
a small lamp from home,
a white ginger jar.

For some reason, I thought
she might need the low light.
I could give her little else

than robins' egg blue
butterflies, light-
winging spirits.

In darkest morning
she might be cold,
but I was the one

who needed to be
tucked in, smoothed.
Through hospital mini-blinds

I thought I saw a circling
of crows—a sign for death
she once told me.

As children we kept a bird
with a yellow top hat
on the windowsill;

its round red beak
dip-dipped into a juice
glass to tell us what

we could already see
for ourselves: heavy
clouds yield rain.

We waited for the doctor's
rounds. There'd be no surprise
conclusions. The clouds

low, expectant. What else
can be made from the labor
of passage? It was this way:

She's gone
said the nurse.
Thank you, I said,

allowed
to worship her then,
her pale freckled skin

and parted lips.
She was still
there in the room

but we didn't care
to speak. Tell me
what isn't death when

life sets its intentions
toward that end? Who'd blame
anyone for counting on

fingers, the math of mortality?
Obstacles set against the need for
comfort played by ear

on black and white keys
a handful of tunes—
Heart and Soul,

Flight of the Bumblebee,
but only the first few
measures. Never the whole song.

You buy grocery store carnations to remind you

how details are important when your work is to usher
the dying. You consider light and its architecture
a means of ascension. You consider sound
a vehicle for passage—the music of footsteps,
of breath. You consider senses in turn, imprints

of the physical world which tend to land you
in flowerbeds. After so many seasons, certain
petals and perfumes call back funerals and hospitals,
apologies that arrive too late for resolution.
But Mother always showed up before
you knew you needed her—like a need

for the warmth of yellow against
February's colorless earth. Every year
it reminds you of the temporary nature
of all that's green. Still, the daffodil is
your favorite flower: stupidly hopeful,
pushing up through the hard earth.

The Company I Keep

I thought I'd outgrow your lullaby,
that long division worked itself out

eventually. With more years
than cakes could hold candles,

I wouldn't need your voice
calling hello, calling me awake

to question every station of the heart.
These pages are you now, Mother:

sorting out the broken bits,
dropping pennies in a jar.

I'll always see your lipsticked
mouth in the moon.

Who can be more than you,
carrying me in your body?

The Way You Still Blame the Dead for Unfinished Business

Maybe if you hadn't started at all,
if the canvas had just been left blank.
Maybe if there'd been no tubes of paint

to salvage from your old habit of unfinished
business, if the colors left had been in hues other
than grief. You sketched your parents, to later study

the light in a photograph your father took with a timer:
American Gothic in the early evening light. Mother
in her work heels, readers perched on her head;

Father in a loosened tie, two pens in his breast pocket,
on the steps of the house they'd suffered to build—
an image of success he hoped to document. First one funeral,

then the other. You found comfort loading
your brush to paint a background: the white tongue
and groove siding, a proud red cross and bible door,

dark windows, geometry you could count on as truth.
Years later, your mother and father wait for burnt umber
and raw sienna, for a fleshing out in forgiveness.

Even dead, my mother is unreasonably difficult to appease

Please understand how I've worked
to reconcile survivor's guilt against
fate or God's plan or whatever you want
to call the way things emerge
from the shadows. For years, I've kept
watch for a sign to justify holding on
to boxes of china and clouded silver

serving pieces. Their stories, exposed
to this atmosphere, have blackened. What
appears on the surface is more than
anyone should bear. Let's take our turn
at comfort, Mother, letting them go
to spaces empty—waiting in some
other daughter's tidy cupboard.

First Aid for Seizures

Take inventory of your serpentine life, the hum of the refrigerator, the kankatank of the washing machine, cartoons blasting from a TV, long- abandoned. Three boys, two cats, a dog, and their ongoing timpani.

But this sound—

A thump; you pause for a long quarter-second before you start upstairs two at a time calling, calling his name.

Step One: Ease your son to the floor.

This has happened before; it can't be happening again.

Step Two: Turn your son gently onto his side. This will help him breathe.

Step Three: Clear the area around your son of anything hard or sharp. This can protect your son from injury.

When he was eighteen months, the specialist at the special hospital told you about a special book that listed all the special information you needed to know about this kind of special condition, this special myoclonic form.

You always hated that word and its heavy permanence. It should mean something unique and lovely but special was not what you wanted for your child. Not your child.

Beautiful and bright like the others.

Step Four: Put something soft and flat, like a folded jacket, under your son's head. Since you will want to be as close to him as possible, you will likely cradle his head in your arms while his limbs twitch and saliva gurgles up his throat.

You will cry and you will say his name over and over and you will also beg God to make it stop.

You'll bargain anything to make it stop.

Step Five: Time the seizure. Call 911 if it lasts longer than 5 minutes. This will be a guess, of course, because no one in the house is looking at his watch; they are all looking at your son. Waiting for it to stop. And it does, but only for a very few seconds before

it will begin again.

After Chemo

Certain subjects I avoid—plans that reach
beyond arms' length, for instance.

Her head—wrapped like a present, pink
bow above the ghost of her left brow.

We are here for sandwiches on fresh bread,
carrot juice, spinach smoothies—organic.

Our words step over sidewalk cracks
like the rhyme we said in school. Once,

we might have complained about gray
roots or sagging breasts, clueless

partners, empty nests; today
we exchange bird stories. How

one was trapped, despite the screen door
propped open. How she worked—

climbing on a rickety table, a rocking
chair, to pluck the wren from

the eaves of her porch, then
release it into a heavy sky.

Tracy Rice Weber is a 2021 graduate of the MFA Program at Old Dominion University. Her poetry has appeared on poets.org, as a recipient of the Academy of American Poets Prize (Graduate). Her poems have also appeared in *Barely South Review, River River,* and *The Bangalore Review,* among others. A former middle and high school teacher, she lives in Virginia on the Peninsula with her husband and sons.

CPSIA information can be obtained
at www.ICGtesting.com
Printed in the USA
LVHW090938240821
695937LV00002B/101